"Captivating, witty, and sensitive. An inspiring book for the ages."

--Marina P. Kennedy, *BroadwayWorld.com*

Father takes six-year-old daughter to see summer production of *Into the Woods* thinking in his ignorance it would be appropriate for children because it's about fairy tales. Problem is that her mother died when daughter was three weeks old, and seeing the show opens the floodgates to almost seven years of unresolved grief for father and daughter both.

Next morning, daughter wakes father and begs him to take her to see it again. And the same the next morning, and the next after that. And so begins a three-week journey into their own dark and scary woods.

*Out of the Woods: A True Story* is about the power of music, theatre and storytelling to open doors and cast light into dark corners. And the power of trust and friendship, as cast members of the show embrace their journey and show how true, life-changing catharsis can happen when you least expect it.

**No One is Alone – Part I**
**Children Will Listen**
From INTO THE WOODS
Words and Music by Stephen Sondheim
© 1988 RILTING MUSIC, INC.
All Rights Administered by WB MUSIC CORP.
All Rights Reserved   Used by Permission
*Reprinted by Permission of Hal Leonard Corporation*

# OUT OF THE WOODS

## A TRUE STORY

*To Linda —*
*There are*
*similar stories*
*traceable back*
*to your*
*teaching!*

*Best,*

## KEVIN FARLEY

The month of August came along, and I had scheduled some time off. For three relaxing weeks, Kendyll and I would live by our whims, free of any concern for the weighty issues of life. Then Labor Day and back to our regular lives of work and the challenges facing a new second grader at Coastal Ridge Elementary School.

One night, I saw a listing for a production by a theatre company in Boston called the Publick Theatre. They did their summer season in a park along the Charles River. The seating wasn't reserved. You could just show up and buy your tickets and see the show. But the thing that caught my interest was that the show was Stephen Sondheim and James Lapine's *Into the Woods*.

I knew almost nothing about musical theatre, but I was familiar with another show by the two. Ten years earlier, just before Leslie and I got married, a friend who worked in theatre gave me the cast album of *Sunday in the Park with George*. The subject matter resonated and the music was challenging and changed all my ideas of what a "show tune" could be. *Into the Woods* came out two years later, and my friend sent me the CD. I put it on top of my pile, but my life was so hectic then, I never got around to listening to it. The CD, still sealed in its wrapping, worked its way down the pile until I eventually packed it away and forgot about it.

I knew *Into the Woods* had fairy tale characters like Cinderella, Jack and the Beanstalk, Little Red Ridinghood, Rapunzel, a Wicked Witch, and a childless Baker and his Wife. I had seen a few seconds of video somewhere that made the show look pretty fun and upbeat, but I troubled to make no further inquiries, nor did my minimal knowledge of theatre allow a responsible assessment of the likelihood of Stephen Sondheim suddenly deciding to do a fun show for kids on Broadway. I take no pride in the fact that it never entered my mind to question whether it would be appropriate for an almost seven-year-old, especially this almost seven-year-old.

But we talked it over, packed our sweaters, bug spray, picnic dinner, and pillows for the ride home, and drove the hour down to Boston to see *Into the Woods*. We got there early. We parked in a lot by some dense woods. We walked a path through a gap in the trees to get in. The theatre was rows of benches in a natural amphitheatre, surrounded by tall trees. The staging and rigging and sets all looked quite impressive.

"Wow, look at this place," I said.

"It's like we're in the woods."

"We are deep in the woods," I said, in my best ominous voice. "And by show time, it'll be getting nice and dark and scary."

Kendyll chose seats way up front. It was all very informal. The audience filtered in while the cast sat around chatting and doing hair and makeup. We looked at the cast bios in the program and talked about little details that stood out. The actor who played Jack had done children's workshops at a theatre up near us in Portsmouth. The Baker's Wife had been in another Sondheim show the previous year with the same director, which seemed like a good sign. Cinderella had gone to Emerson College, which had been all over the news recently when they almost relocated outside of Boston, and we had some fun discussing the challenges of moving a college.

The cast took the stage to warm up with vocal

exercises. There must have been at least twenty of them in their bright, colorful costumes, and they sounded fantastic and sang louder and louder until you could feel the sound hit you in the chest. The musicians warmed up, juicing up the excitement with little horn fanfares, drum rolls, ripples of flute and piano. The lighting crew sent spots back and forth and flipped through different scenes. As the feeling of anticipation reached its excruciating peak, I took a glance at Kendyll. She sat wide-eyed, taking it all in, practically shaking with excitement. I looked at her beaming face and felt a warm glow of self-regard. Kendyll was indeed lucky to have such a diligent father.

\*\*\*

At eight o'clock, twilight was falling and the show began. The prologue was epic in proportion and the music was like a roller coaster. Half a dozen story lines were laid out at dizzying speed, careening back and forth between a bunch of different characters. The pieces all fit together like an intricate puzzle, and you'd miss vital information if you so much as blinked. The performances and production values were amazing, and Kendyll and I were thoroughly engrossed.

I noticed there were a lot of loving mothers. We watched Cinderella receive guidance, as well as a very spiffy gown and pair of slippers, from the spirit of her mother, embodied in a tree at her grave. We watched Jack's mother struggle to show patience with the son she was raising alone and in poverty. We were charmed by the feisty Red Ridinghood's devotion to her Granny. And we felt the longing of the Baker and his Wife for a child of their own. We even felt sympathy for the Witch as she tried to protect her daughter Rapunzel from the evils of the world.

During intermission, we had drinks and snacks.

"It's *so* great, Dad!"

"Isn't it incredible? And it's funny!"

"It's exciting!"

"The scene when they lifted the spell was too exciting. My heart's still pounding."

"But Dad, how come everybody got their wish except the Baker and his Wife?"

"They'll get their wish. She's pregnant. Remember

when she patted her tummy and thanked Cinderella for the slipper?"

"Oh, okay!"

We chatted on excitedly until the dimming lights summoned us back for the second act. We took our seats, and I whispered to Kendyll, "Are you ready?"

"Ready!"

We settled back, but within a minute or two the atmosphere took a sharp turn as the Giant's Wife comes rampaging down the beanstalk to avenge the death of her husband. The Baker and his Wife's home is destroyed, and Red Ridinghood shows up and says the same with her house and that her mother is missing. Then, in rapid succession: the Narrator dies, Rapunzel dies, Jack's mother dies, Cinderella learns of the destruction of the tree at her mother's grave, the Baker's Wife dies, the Baker learns of her death, Red learns of her Granny's death, and the Baker freaks out at the idea that he is now a widower with an infant to raise. He panics and flees into the woods, leaving his baby in the care of Cinderella. He encounters the spirit of his dead father, who tells how he tried to run away from his troubles when his wife died, and he doesn't want the

Baker to make the same mistake.

The Baker sings a song called "No More," a raw expression of grief and anguish by a man overwhelmed by events. I started to feel something almost like panic rising up from somewhere, like I couldn't believe what was happening, and the intense emotions I was feeling about a story I knew wasn't real were spilling into areas of my own life and experience that I knew were real, and triggering a flood of images from the past until I somehow got confused to the point where I guess I started thinking the story might be real, too.

Part of my problem was the way that last part of the show is structured. There are very few breaks in the action as in a traditional show. A lot of songs don't really end, but roll right into the next song or the next scene. A few just abruptly stop, when some sudden development yanks the story away in another direction. The continuous action, along with my compromised emotional state, was like some kind of massive 3D musical theatre Hypno-Disc, drawing me deeper and deeper into the story.

It turned out the show was almost over at that point, although the worst was still to come. Cinderella sits with

Red and sings her a song called "No One is Alone," the show's high-water mark of gut-wrench, an unbearably beautiful melody, sung with exquisite tenderness to a poor grieving kid about how her mother can't guide her and now she's on her own.

I sat with my arm around Kendyll and stared at the ground, unable to look at the stage, suspended in disbelief, but not any willing kind of disbelief. Then I felt her shaking, and looked up to see her staring back at me, hollow-eyed, with tears streaming down her face. The wave of emotion welling up inside me finally broke the surface. My eyes filled with tears as I held Kendyll, and wiped her tears with napkins from my backpack under my seat. And I gathered my strength and forced that wave of memories back down into the depths.

Then we came to my personal highlight: the Baker, lost and bewildered, holding the baby while having a lovely conversation with the spirit of his departed Wife, who says he can be both mother and father and that he'll know what to do. Then one last devastating fragment of "No One is Alone," sung this time by the Baker's Wife as she offers him solace and encouragement:

**Sometimes people leave you
halfway through the wood.
Do not let it grieve you,
No one leaves for good.**

Finally she tells the Baker to hold the baby to the light so he can see "the glow." Then another song called "Children Will Listen," that led into the finale. There must have been an ending of some kind in there, too. But I think by then both Kendyll and I were too numb to process much new information. We finally just kind of looked around and realized the show was over.

We gathered our belongings, tossed our clump of soggy napkins in a trash can, and dragged ourselves out to the car. We were both completely shell-shocked. We drove in silence until we were well out of the city, out on the dark highway, with few other cars around. My mind was racing, trying to absorb what we had seen. It seemed obvious that I should say something, but I couldn't think of anything that could possibly do justice to the situation. I kept glancing over at Kendyll, hoping maybe she would fall asleep. But she stared straight ahead, frowning in concentration. She looked like a kid with a lot on her mind. Suddenly, she spoke up.

"Dad? The Baker saw his father in the woods when he ran away."

"Yes."

"I don't understand why his father would tell him it's a good idea to run away."

"Well, he said it, but he didn't really mean it. He was making a point, like he's playing along, saying sure go ahead and run away, but where were you thinking of going? Trying to get the Baker to calm down and think about what he's doing."

"What was he doing?"

"He just said he was going away."

"But where?"

"He didn't think that far ahead. I think his fear got the better of him. Right at the beginning, his wife says he's fearful of the woods at night."

"When they went to get the stuff for the spell?"

"Right," I said. "Although he wanted her to stay safe at home while he went. Which is pretty brave."

"And he was really brave when he saved Red and Granny from the Wolf."

"He sure was. If he was afraid, he didn't let it stop him. And he doesn't know it yet, but he'll figure out how to take care of a baby. People have been doing it for years. You'd be amazed at who can figure it out."

I looked over to see if Kendyll was appreciating the subtlety of my wit, but her eyes were starting to close. When we got home, she never stirred as I carried her in to bed.

\*\*\*

"Dad? Can we go see *Into the Woods* tonight?"

My eyes popped open after a fitful night's sleep. Kendyll had skipped into my room and planted a kiss on my cheek. She was awfully perky for a kid who'd been out until after midnight, not to mention the part about having her guts ripped out by the very same show just nine hours before.

"Please Dad, can we go tonight?"

"You're not serious, are you?"

"Dad."

"Kendyll. It was so upsetting. Why would you want to?"

"Dad, please!" she cried. "I just really think we should go!"

I looked into her eyes and recognized a glint of determination that I knew well. It had popped up at different times in Kendyll's life: right before she took her first steps, or went down the big slide, or prepared for the first time to heft her backpack up that big first step on the school bus.

"I don't really understand this," I thought. "But if I tell her no, what do I give her for a reason?"

I persuaded her two late nights in a row might be a little taxing, but how about the following night. We spent the morning cleaning the house and taking the dog up to the woods, and Kendyll went to a friend's house for the afternoon. Then we had dinner and took a bike ride. As soon as Kendyll was asleep, I headed for my office and started rummaging around in a pile of boxes stacked in the closet.

I found the box I wanted, and fished out my long-forgotten CD of *Into the Woods*. I unwrapped it and took it into the living room. I stretched out on the couch with my disc player, and put on the headphones. I came to a song called "It Takes Two," where the Baker and his Wife are feeling optimistic and confident as they sing about their love and partnership and how much they depend on each other, and how by acting together they can dispel an evil curse and realize their dream of having a child. I found myself remembering a long-ago December night. Leslie and I had been married almost three years. She came home from work one night looking like she had been crying.

"What's wrong?"

"I don't even want to tell you."

"What do you mean?"

"I had this weird dream the other night that I was having a baby, and there was a big storm and it got really dark and I was stuck alone somewhere, and I couldn't find you, and it was like a real nightmare. Then I had it again last night."

"You didn't say anything."

"I didn't want to you to worry I was going to spring 'hey, let's suddenly have a baby' on you. I know we're not ready. The house needs so much work."

Tears filled her eyes.

"I'm really sorry," she said. "I don't know what's wrong with me. I just keep waking up and feeling like something could go wrong."

So we talked and decided things happen for a reason, and that we would always try to follow our hunches, and who's ever ready for a baby anyway, and maybe it was time to revise our plan about the right time to have a baby.

*** 

"Did you sleep on the couch, Dad?"

I tried to lift my head, but the headphone cable was wrapped around my neck.

"What time should we leave tonight?"

"Are you really sure?"

"Dad!"

So that evening, we packed our stuff and drove to Boston. I was feeling a little apprehensive, but Kendyll was all business and utterly determined that we get there in a timely manner and see that show.

"Should we listen to the traffic, Dad?"

"We can, but I'm pretty sure we're good."

We arrived early, and took our same seats in front. We knew what was coming this time so the shock value was obviously reduced. We had a few emotional moments, but were both completely absorbed in the action from beginning to end. The main difference was when we knew a wallop was coming up we instinctively reached out to hold each other.

We came to the scene where the Baker has learned of his Wife's death and the characters are taking stock of their situation. The Baker in his anger tells Jack the whole mess is his fault because he was responsible for the beanstalk, and Jack replies that he got the beans from the Baker in the first place. One thing leads to another and the characters break into a song called "Your Fault," a rollicking, fast-paced free-for-all of blame, sung in rapid interchange by Jack, the Baker, Red, the Witch, and Cinderella. The song is like a five-way ping-pong game using guilt for a ball, and it moves along at a furious pace. I took a glance at Kendyll to see if she seemed able to follow it. She wore an expression of utmost concentration, head nodding, looking back and forth as the characters volleyed accusations at each other.

On the drive home, we were quiet again until we were out on the highway. Then Kendyll spoke up as abruptly as she had the first night.

"Now, Dad? The Baker blamed Jack for the beanstalk."

"Yes."

"But Jack got the beans from him."

"Exactly."

"And he had them because his father stole them from the garden and left them in the jacket?"

"Right."

"Did he know his father stole them? Because the Witch was really mad about it, right?"

"That's why she laid the spell in the first place."

"Oh, wait," said Kendyll. "His father told him when they were in the woods."

"Right. He said he thought it was okay at the time, because he meant them as a gift for his wife."

"Isn't that like Jack stealing the hen and saying it was for his mother?" Kendyll asked.

"Exactly. They both thought they were justified in what

they did. They acted without thinking, and later tried to come up with excuses. The only one who really kept her head during the whole thing was the Witch. She totally acted like a witch, but at least she was always thinking straight."

"She did lock Rapunzel in the tower, though," said Kendyll. "And kind of messed up her life."

"You're right."

"And you know who else, Dad? The Baker's Wife. She lied about the beans when she traded them to Jack. Well, I mean she lied when she said they were magic even though they were, because she didn't know it."

I burst out laughing.

"Wow, Kendyll! You're really paying attention to this thing, aren't you? You could be like a fairy tale lawyer!"

We drove on, pondering these weighty issues of life, and Kendyll soon dropped off to sleep. And, like the first night, she was a dead weight in my arms as I carried her in to bed. I took the dog out and gave her a treat and grabbed my disc player and headed for the couch. I was at the beginning of Act II.

Cinderella has her prince and is seemingly happy living

in the palace. Jack and his mother are wealthy and content. The Baker and his Wife at last have a child. They all sing about how perfect everything is and how they never thought they could be so happy. But the song is cut off by sudden disaster as the enraged Giant's Wife comes crashing down the beanstalk.

I was in a hotel room. Fifteen minutes earlier, I had called home and gotten the answering machine for the third time in an hour. It was a little unsettling because Leslie was about halfway to term and had an appointment with her obstetrician that afternoon. We had planned to talk before I went to work. I was getting ready to head out when the phone rang.

"It's me."

"Where are you? I've been calling home."

"Don't freak out, but I'm in the hospital."

"What happened?"

"On my way to see Linda, I got this jolt of pain in my head, and I got there, and she took me next door to a neurologist, and they walked me across the hall to an ophthalmologist, and he looked in my eyes, and the next thing I knew they were checking me in to the hospital."

"What's going on?"

"It sounds scary, but it's not. It's a benign inter-cranial tumor. It's like a blood clot that bled a little."

"Like a stroke? You had a stroke?"

"It's not a stroke. The clot didn't move or anything."

"How about the baby?"

"She's fine. She's on a monitor, and she's fine."

"How do you feel?"

"I have a headache, but they gave me something."

"How long are they keeping you?"

"Well, it looks like I'm having surgery tomorrow afternoon."

*"What?"*

"They think they can pop the whole thing out in an hour or so, and I can go home in a few days."

"I'll see if there's a flight tonight. I'm right by the airport."

"Wait, Kevin. Could you really get out of there tonight? And what about the car? Meg and Dave took the dog to their house, so she's okay. My mom and my sister are here. You can't cancel without any notice. Why not do your show and get your check and drive home in the morning?"

"I guess you do sound okay. Are you sure, though?"

"It's going to be fine. Nothing will happen here until tomorrow."

The surgery didn't happen and the doctors decided to keep Leslie in the hospital to keep an eye on things. She had a small spot of blurred vision, but she was stable and the baby was okay. They were thinking AVM, arteriovenous malformation, a mass of distorted circulatory tissue, probably congenital, stressed by hormones and elevated blood pressure from the pregnancy. A true diagnosis would have to wait because of pregnancy-related limitations on diagnostic radiology. But we were given to understand that this bleeding could be a fortunate alert to danger, because otherwise the AVM could have gone undetected and caused a stroke during labor.

Leslie came home after a few days, and I returned to work. One night, she lost her balance and fell and wound up back in the hospital. There were problems getting her pain under control and she kept having trouble with her balance, so the game plan was to be extra cautious. Leslie resigned herself to staying in the hospital for the rest of the summer. As soon as the baby was far enough along, she would have a C-Section, rest a few days, have the AVM popped out, and we'd all go home.

*\*\**

"Dad? Can we go see *Into the Woods* tonight?"

"Are you kidding me?"

"Please, Dad?"

"Why?"

"There's more stuff to figure out!"

"We talked about going two nights in a row. I can't keep you out late every night."

"Can we go tomorrow night?"

"Well, after tonight they're off until Thursday."

"But, Dad. It's only Sunday. If we went tonight we'd have three whole days to rest."

My rule with her was always that she could try to make her case, and it seemed that she kind of had a point with that one.

We arrived that night and took our seats, and the actress who played Red Ridinghood came over and sat down a couple of seats from Kendyll.

"Hi," she said. "You seem like a real fan of the show."

"Oh, I am!" Kendyll said.

"Are you interested in acting?"

"Oh, yes!"

"I thought you might be," Red replied. "By the way, I'm Susan."

We introduced ourselves.

"What do you think of Red?" I asked.

"She's a total brat," Susan replied. "And I love her."

"She's pretty fun."

"I know. She says outrageous things. I want to be like her when I grow up. Except maybe for the pulling a knife on people."

"Did you do acting when you were little?" asked Kendyll.

"I did. My mother was an actress, and she would rehearse around the house and I just always took to it. Have you done any acting or performing, Kendyll?"

"A little bit. At school, and some dance recitals, and a show we do in our town at Christmas time."

"Good for you. I can totally picture you up on a stage dazzling everybody. I'm sure you're a natural."

Kendyll beamed.

"Well," said Susan. "I guess I better get back. It's great to meet you guys."

We made it through the performance pretty well, and eventually came to the scene near the end where Red's bold front finally crumbles under her grief and she begins to cry. Cinderella comforts her and they talk about Red's concern that her mother and Granny wouldn't be proud of her. Kendyll let out a deep sigh, and I pulled her close as tears came to her eyes.

After the performance, we headed out and drove in silence for a while, as Kendyll stared out the window with furrowed brow. Then, with her usual lack of preamble, she spoke up.

"Dad. Red is a funny one."

"How so?"

"The first thing she does is ask for bread and treats for her Granny, and then takes it all and stuffs her face with it."

"Yup," I said, laughing.

"Then when the Baker tries to take the cape, she makes this big scene about it and he's so ashamed he brings it back. And then she stomps on his foot. She's tough, Dad.

27

She took her knife and tried to attack the Giant's Wife."

"She was pretty worked up about her mother and Granny."

"But Dad. She's not really a bad person. She gave the Baker her cape to thank him for saving her and Granny. He and his wife couldn't have lifted the spell without it. And when they were talking about handing Jack over to the Giant's Wife, Red was really upset."

"You're right. She's interesting. She's this hothead who might pull a knife on you, but she always does the right thing when it really matters."

"She took care of the baby when the Baker and his Wife went to look for Jack."

"She did. And she was really torn on the question of killing the Giant's Wife. She was worried her mother and Granny would be disappointed in her for not showing forgiveness."

"Yeah, Dad. Susan's right. Red's just kind of a punk."

"I think so, too. So what's up with the attitude, do you think?"

"Maybe she's really scared, but she doesn't want to show it, so she's trying to act big?"

"Wow, Kendyll. How old are you again?"

We drove on a little while.

"You know," I said. "Red lost her whole family. Of course she's upset. When she went after the Giant's Wife, she was in a rage. 'It's because of you I've no mother!' and all that. It's kind of a well-known thing that when people have a loss like that, they'll have a lot of different feelings, and anger is one of them. Remember how harsh the Baker was before he ran away? That's an angry guy. Such a big loss would leave some kind of mark. As we know pretty well ourselves, right?"

"I guess so. But we were just a Dad and a baby, too. And we're doing okay."

"Of course we are. I think we're doing great."

We drove on a bit and I considered Kendyll's opinion that she and I were doing okay. The early days of our life together didn't seem so promising. I understood I had work to do. I read about the stages of grief, except I misunderstood and thought they were like homework assignments instead of a description of a highly variable natural process. I tried my best at denial, with disappointing results. The circumstances I lived with every day seemed pretty undeniable. I had conveniently forgotten that my first fleeting thought the moment I finally learned where Leslie's situation was leading was that they must have mixed up the files.

As for anger, I decided it didn't apply to me because there was no one to be angry at. There was no one to blame for what happened to Leslie, so I must have figured I could skip that assignment. It struck me in no way peculiar that I was in a rage about everything else. I walked out of a big family Christmas dinner at a nice restaurant because I had an old grudge against the owners and there was a minor issue with the food. I quit a band in the middle of a rehearsal and left them in the lurch for a show we had booked. I had a heated public confrontation with the town manager about a tree in the town right-of-way that fell in a storm and damaged my house. All this perceived injustice became a slow drip of rage, and it got worse, too.

A guy cut me off when I was turning onto the highway, and I chased him at high speed trying to pull ahead of him so I could cut him off in retaliation, endangering me and him and other drivers. Not to mention my precious and vulnerable baby daughter sleeping next to me in her car seat. That was the night I called a child abuse hotline and asked them for a checklist of warning signs, as if I needed it. The person on the other end of the line was wonderful and we talked for quite a while, and the crisis eventually passed without obvious harm to Kendyll. But, as she grew older, I knew I was too demanding of her, and lacked patience with her. And my bitterness continued to fester beneath the surface. My relationships with my family and Leslie's family and many of my friends suffered for it. A couple of close friends tried to bring up the subject, and I brushed them off on the basis that they hadn't been through it, and couldn't know what it was like. And I didn't bother to be nice about it, either. I was resentful instead of grateful, and all it did was add fuel to my rage.

I had spent the ten years before Kendyll came along travelling around the country, building an audience, playing with amazing people and making good money. My new situation meant drastically cutting back and trying to start something that didn't require travel. I gave no thought to the conversations I'd had with Leslie about the ways in which we'd have to adjust to parenthood, and that my old days of travelling all over the place were numbered anyway. I managed to hang onto a couple of my old jobs. There was a place just outside Philadelphia, probably my favorite place to play ever. I'd do a four-night week there every couple of months. I'd pack the car and put Kendyll in her car seat and drive seven hours to the homes of friends who took her in and made her a part of their families while I worked. She was a brave and dauntless travelling companion during these years, happily carrying her little backpack up the walk to the Graf's or O'Callaghan's or Durkin's house. We'd have dinner, and I'd go off to play the gig, leaving her cuddling with my friends' kids to hear a bedtime story. I can only imagine what an imposition I must have been to these wonderful, generous people, especially considering my surly attitude toward the world at the time. But nobody ever gave any hint of it. Of course, this situation could only last until Kendyll started kindergarten, and I left this last vestige of my old life behind.

Back home, I scraped together a living doing gigs in local places for a fraction of what I had made before. I had exactly one gig I liked doing, and it was one night a week during the summer. I felt like I was above those other places, and people picked up on it, and soon even those jobs started getting harder to come by. I was too defiant to consider going back to school or finding a new line of work that was more compatible with my new responsibilities.

I thought of those early days, as Kendyll and I drove on home through the night. I felt very lucky she thought we were okay, because there were times when it could have gone either way.

The next night, we went to the high school and knocked some tennis balls around with my sister Meg and her kids, and came home and did our usual bedtime reading. Once Kendyll was asleep, I headed straight to the couch, put on my headphones, and picked up listening.

The Baker and his Wife, Jack, Red, and Cinderella are reluctantly returning to the woods to deal with the threat presented by the angry Giant's Wife. I pictured the characters peering fearfully around as fog creeps across the stage, and the music goes to a spooky minor-key version of the show's main theme, and the woods get darker and scarier.

The hospital had finagled things so Leslie had a private room. I brought furniture from home and decorated with family pictures and art posters. I brought in books, magazines, videos, CDs, a VCR, and stereo system. They let us put party hats and sunglasses on various pieces of medical equipment. We settled into a routine. Meg and Dave kept the dog. A pay phone in the hospital vending room served as my office. I slept on a foam pad on the floor, showered and kept a few changes of clothes in Leslie's bathroom, going off to work, stopping at home every few days for mail and laundry and lawn mowing.

We entertained ourselves by drawing all over an enlarged photocopied cross-section of the regions of the brain. We turned the brain into an elaborate pirate's treasure map, an island with an "X" where Leslie's blood clot supposedly was, and a picture of a treasure chest. We drew little icons in different spots and matched them to clues at the bottom of the page. We enlisted visiting friends and family and hospital staff in the effort. Bad puns were the order of the day. We had a mountain range called the Scalps, and another called the Sierra Bellums.

"This could be a board game," Leslie said. "Let's get rich this summer by inventing a board game."

Meg brought our dog Ceili to the hospital. I wheeled

Leslie outside and the dog went wild with joy.

"How's my girl?" Leslie said, laughing as Ceili jumped into her lap, yelping and licking her face. "How's my girl?"

Every couple of days, I watched the dog leap with joy at seeing Leslie. She threw a frisbee for Ceili to catch and retrieve, and, every time, I felt relief that things seemed to be going according to plan.

\*\*\*

The next night, as Kendyll and I bought our tickets, the box office manager said, "How are you two this evening?"

"Oh, fine," we said.

"My name's Karen," she said, sticking out her hand. "What's yours?"

"Kendyll."

"What a pretty name. How do you spell it?"

Kendyll spelled it out, and we exchanged a few more pleasantries and took our seats. About ten minutes later, Karen came out from backstage with a program for Kendyll, autographed by the cast.

"Wow, thank you! Look, Dad!"

We looked over all the signatures, and a few minutes later, Susan came out with the actor who played Jack.

"Hey, guys," she said. "This is Sean. He wanted to say hi."

"Susan says you're from Maine," Sean said. "I worked in Portsmouth for a while."

"We saw that in the program. Who did you work with?"

We talked a little bit about people we knew in Portsmouth and Sean's interest in variety and circus performance, and he went off to greet some arriving friends.

A few minutes later, we heard voices from behind us.

"Hey, Bob. Isn't that the famous Kendyll over there?"

We turned and saw The Baker and his Wife, sitting a few rows behind us.

"Hi, Kendyll!" said the Baker's Wife. "I'm Maryann. This is Bob. Do you think he'll remember his lines for a change tonight?"

"I keep pretty busy covering for her," said Bob.

Maryann and Bob were both very well established in Boston area theatre. They seemed to be good friends, and you could tell they were comfortable working together.

They bantered back and forth a little more, and got up to head backstage. They stopped by our seats on the way.

"Good to see you two," said Bob.

"You two work really well together," I said.

"We do depend on each other," said Maryann. "He's always there for me."

"Hey," I said. "No one is alone!"

They smiled and rolled their eyes. Bob turned to Kendyll, and gestured toward me with his thumb.

"You live with this guy?"

"I sure do," Kendyll said, giggling.

"That sounds tough, Kendyll," said Maryann. "But at least he takes you to a lot of shows."

We were laughing at this comment when Cinderella came out, and Maryann called to her, "Molly, come meet Kendyll and Kevin!"

Molly had a warm, enthusiastic personality that kind of reminded me of Cinderella.

"It's nice to meet you both," she said. "I'm really glad you've taken such an interest in the show. It's a wonderful show, isn't it?"

"I guess we're pretty caught up in it," I replied.

"That's probably okay."

By now we were getting through the show mostly unscathed. We came to Cinderella's solo song, "On the Steps of the Palace." It's a song of circumspection, doubt and definite misgivings, as Cinderella struggles between being true to herself and riding the wave of her wish coming true. Then later, we came to the scene where Cinderella discovers that her mother's tree has fallen, and that her hopes have been crushed. She's in disguise, but the Baker realizes she's the Princess and falls to his knees.

"Get up!" she says, clearly uncomfortable. "I'm not a Princess here."

On the way home, Kendyll again said nothing until we were out on the highway. She stared out into the darkness as usual, and I felt like I could almost hear the wheels turning in her brain.

"Dad? You never hear anything more about Cinderella's mother. What happened to her?"

"I'm not sure, but Cinderella was crying like she knew she had really lost her mother."

"Wasn't she like a spirit?"

"That's what I thought."

We drove on a while. Kendyll stared out the window. Finally she spoke up.

"She lived in the tree, but she was separate from it, right? You wouldn't hurt a spirit if you just knocked down their tree."

"I don't think so either."

"So why would her tree being lost make her be lost too?"

"That's a good question. Like why not just find another tree?"

"Cinderella would have to figure out where the new tree was, though."

"Ever the practical one, Kendyll. But when you create a whole world like they do in this show, you have to have rules to make it interesting. It's like having a net in tennis. Or the Witch not being allowed to touch the ingredients for the potion. Like where did that come from?"

"So maybe she only got one tree?"

"Sounds like it, doesn't it? Cinderella never talks about trying to find her or anything."

"No."

"Cinderella is a brave soul, Kendyll. First she's

practically held prisoner by her Stepmother and those nasty stepsisters, but still keeps her cheerful nature. And now she finds the ruins of her mother's grave and is there weeping when the Baker comes along and says, like by the way, your castle's been wrecked and your family are now refugees in the woods trying to get to some hidden kingdom. Oh, and they don't know where your prince is, either. I think Cinderella's had the hardest time of anybody."

"And she's the nicest, too," replied Kendyll. "When the Baker went to the palace to tell them about the giant, the guard guy was really snobby to him, but she treated him with respect. And even when she dumped her prince, she wasn't mean to him."

"She was nicer than he deserved. I think Cinderella's the coolest person of them all. She knew who she was and was comfortable with it. She knew in her heart she'd never feel at home in a palace. And you're right; she did everything she could to help other people. Even the little birds loved her because she was kind to them and called them her friends. You'd think little birds would have some pretty good intuition about who's kind and gentle and who's not."

"She took care of Red and Jack, too," said Kendyll. "The only time she thought of herself was when she wanted to go to the ball."

"That is really a great point. Even when she was grieving for her mother, she comforted Red when she lost her Granny. Remember in the very beginning, when she says she tried to be good and kind like her mother taught her? She totally does that. She always acts in a way that would make her mother proud."

We drove on a while longer, and off Kendyll went to sleep. I carried her in to bed as usual, and took care of the dog. Then I hurried into the living room, and got my CD player. I knew the show well enough by now to pause between songs and fill in the action from memory. I came to where the Baker finds his Wife's scarf on the ground and the Witch tells him of her death. I thought of the disbelief on the Baker's face, like he was thinking maybe it was all some kind of mistake. He sings "No More," clutching the scarf to his chest. And I couldn't get that scarf out of my mind as I played and replayed the song, drawn farther into my memories of a life slipping out of control.

Leslie's pain was getting worse. The blurry spot in her vision was growing. Her spinal fluid wasn't re-circulating properly and was building up and causing pressure. Frequent spinal taps worked for a while to drain the fluid. But soon, they couldn't keep ahead of it, and a team of neurosurgeons entered the picture and decided to install a plastic tube from between layers of cranial membrane down into her stomach to shunt off the excess fluid, where it would quickly be rendered harmless by digestive acids. It was pretty simple, as neurosurgical procedures go, but it did require a head shave.

Meg brought Ceili over a few days later, and I wheeled Leslie out to toss the frisbee. I guess her scent was obscured by all the medications and constant applications of pungent disinfectants. Her shaved head must have confused Ceili even more. She ran up to Leslie, took one sniff, and ran off in the other direction. My efforts to focus her attention on Leslie failed, and Meg took her home. Leslie cried as I wheeled her back into the hospital.

"She doesn't know me!"

"She's just excited. You probably smell different."

"It's my hair, too. I think she's starting to forget about

me."

"She won't forget about you. She's just confused."

"I must be changing a lot."

"No, you're not. You're doing okay."

But she wasn't doing okay. Her balance deteriorated and her reflexes started to fail. The shunt couldn't keep up, and her weight plunged when she couldn't eat or drink anything due to the pressure from the excess fluid. Obviously there was something going on, but there was no safe way to find out what it was until the baby was delivered. The idea was to wait until the baby would be able to breathe on her own, but tests showed she wasn't there yet. Out in the hallway, the neurosurgical and obstetric camps held urgent, whispered debates.

"Leslie's symptoms are worsening. But the baby is still showing pulmonary insufficiency. She will need to go right into a level three neonatal intensive care unit. Then we'll need to turn Leslie around as quickly as possible, and get her into surgery. We think it would be best to send her to Boston, where they're equipped to really go at this."

The tipping point was reached on a Friday night in September. I followed in my car as Leslie was driven to

Boston by the same ambulance crew from her first hospital transfer.

By midnight, I was holding Kendyll in my arms. She was tiny and beautiful, with spiky hair the color of a brand new penny. To everyone's surprise, she was breathing fine on her own, so she needed only a few days in the ICU to get her weight up.

At seven o'clock Monday morning, the neurosurgery team went to work. I spent the day jogging the ten minutes back and forth between the surgical waiting room and the pediatric ICU in another building. I was in the grip of some hero complex about being the one who gave Kendyll her bottle and changed her diapers, so I'd run and do that, and then hurry back to sit by the phone to the operating room.

The surgery went fourteen hours. At ten o'clock that night, I put on a cap and gown and paper booties, and followed a nurse through a maze of deserted recovery bays to say good night.

"Right around this corner," the nurse murmured.

We stepped into the recovery bay, and I felt a chill. Leslie was asleep. Her head was heavily bandaged, and was attached to a metal frame with giant screws that seemed to extend through the bandages into her skull.

"Can I kiss?" I whispered.

"Of course," the nurse said.

I leaned to kiss her on the cheek and felt that chill again. I moved around so she could see me. She opened her eyes, but it was a struggle.

"You did it," I whispered. "You got through it great."

She opened her mouth to talk but couldn't form words.

"Kendyll had a great day. She's breathing fine and she's regaining weight. I'll bring her to you in the morning. I'll bet we'll all be home in no time."

Leslie moved her lips and made a sound. I leaned closer.

"What was that?"

She took a breath and tried again.

"No."

\*\*\*

Kendyll and I went to see *Into the Woods* every Thursday, Saturday, and Sunday night for the next two weeks. We were obsessed. We knew almost every line and lyric. We played the CD in the house, and I made a cassette to play in the car as we drove around doing errands and such. We learned the words to a bunch of the songs by sheer repetition and sang along. In the car I mean. Not at the show. Kendyll did a rendition of Red's solo number, "I Know Things Now," a song with a lot of tricky rhymes and intervals, and I must say without prejudice that she sounded pretty darn good. We spoke in a secret code of *Into the Woods* allusions and quotations, working favorite lines into our everyday conversations with the outside world. It was like our new covert lifestyle.

We visited beforehand with the cast, mostly Susan, Sean, Maryann, Bob and Molly, but got to know several others too. We talked about the content of the show sometimes, but other times just chatted about whatever. We accumulated stories: the night a sudden thunderstorm washed out a performance just as it was getting started, or the night with the power failure, or the time vandals broke into a storage locker and stole a couple of microphones and the performance was delayed while they rigged replacements, or the night the news helicopter from the TV station across the street inexplicably came and hovered over the stage for a minute or so, completely stopping the show, while the Witch made futile magic gestures with her walking stick. All this shared experience got to a point where it started to feel like we all worked in the same office or played on a team together or something.

We arrived one night to find Maryann and Bob sitting together going over some notes.

"Kendyll," said Maryann. "Will you please convince Bob that it's Jack's Mother who actually throws away the beans?"

"Yes," said Kendyll. "She says 'only a dolt would exchange a cow for beans!'"

"See?" Maryann said. "You really pay attention, don't you, Kendyll?"

"Yes, I do," said Kendyll.

"Hey," I chimed in. "Children will listen!"

Maryann and Bob groaned. Maryann reached down and patted Kendyll on the arm.

"Kendyll," she said. "I'll bet you understand this show better than a lot of grownups who come to it. And we really appreciate it."

"We even appreciate you bringing your Dad," said Bob

with a smile.

Susan and Sean came out to say hi. Susan and Kendyll went off to meet Jack's Mother and Rapunzel, and I asked Sean what he thought of the show and he said he thought it was complex. I said I thought it was a show with ambitions.

"It's about big issues for sure," he said. "But sometimes they drive them home pretty hard."

"They do," I said "But in a fairy tale it's pretty normal to hit people over the head with the moral of the story."

"Good point," said Sean. "I was at a wedding one time and somebody said they thought the minister was preachy. And I thought, 'he's a *minister*.'"

We talked a little more, and Sean headed back. Then Karen from the box office appeared at my side and glanced around and said, "Hey, Kevin? I hope you don't mind me saying this, but everybody is curious about you and Kendyll."

She hesitated, looked over at Kendyll chatting with Susan and the actress who played Jack's Mother.

"Would it be intruding to ask if something happened to her mother?"

I couldn't think of any reason not to, so I gave her the

one-sentence version.

"Would you mind if I told the cast?" she asked.

"I guess not," I replied.

She went backstage, and soon the cast began to gather to warm up. From their whispering and sympathetic looks, I surmised that Karen might have said something. And there certainly was a lovely gentleness in their greetings to Kendyll.

Molly came over to us.

"Hi, you two. Can I sit for a second?"

"Of course."

Molly sat down by Kendyll.

"So, you're liking the show?"

"Oh, yes."

Molly hesitated.

"Some of the songs are kind of intense, aren't they, Kendyll?"

Kendyll nodded.

"Yeah."

Molly leaned down, and spoke very gently, barely above a whisper.

"You know, Kendyll, a song can mean so much to a

person, and really shed light on things for them. And we all try to sing every song like that could be the case for somebody. And if it is, we hope the person really hears it. And sometimes I see someone and I feel like they're really listening. And, when that happens, it reminds me of why I wanted to do this in the first place. I really want to thank you. I'm so glad you and your dad are a part of this show."

She and Kendyll exchanged a hug, and Molly went up to get ready to sing. Susan came by and stopped by our seats.

"Hey, kid," she said to Kendyll. "How are you?"

"Good," said Kendyll.

Susan leaned down and reached out, and Kendyll took her hands.

"You're a special girl, Kendyll," she whispered. "I see wonderful things in store for you."

The performance began, and cast never sounded better. We were fine through the show and came to the scene at the end where the Baker has concluded his conversation with his spirit-tree wife, and is holding the baby and telling the story like his wife said, and repeating the show's opening lines.

"Once upon a time in a far-off kingdom."

He sounds tentative and mournful, in direct contrast with the same words spoken by the dynamic Narrator when he opened the show. Simultaneously, the Witch starts to sing "Children Will Listen," the show's valedictory, a moment of summing up, the one where you are deposited back in the real world and get a minute to sort through the various morals of the story before the big rousing finale.

First the Witch says be careful what you say because children will listen. And no matter what you say, they'll be watching too. And your kids may let you down once in a while, but don't worry too much because all along they have been absorbing the daily lessons of your example. Unless that's something to worry about, of course.

Then the entire company sang, quietly at first, about being careful when you make a wish or cast a spell because they can both get away from you. The lights came up and the music came up and suddenly they were moving forward, all singing in glorious full voice, and little chiming bell sounds started twinkling here and there like shafts of sunlight touching earth after a stormy night, and the whole sound of the music brightened and kept building up, and the lights came up more and turned kind of golden and the whole effect is one of lifting and ascending until our hardy characters in their posture and facial expressions are completely transformed from timid and battered survivors into proud and resolute survivors who went into the dark and scary woods and came out stronger and better for it.

Then it's right into the finale, which is maybe two minutes long, but they do manage to generate enough good energy to send you out feeling not completely devastated. It's like they knock you down, then cheerfully help you up. By this time, we had learned to navigate the emotional currents of the show and, by the end, were still in shape to actually enjoy the end.

On our ride home, Kendyll observed our unspoken 'no talking until we're out on the highway' rule.

"Hey, Dad? You know how Nani says be careful what you wish for?"

"Sure. Because you just might get it."

"That's just like 'careful the wish you make.'"

"Right. They say 'wishes are children.' You bring them into the world and you do your best but you can't control them or predict what they're going to do. You can make some wish that has results that make you wish you had left well enough alone."

"You know, Dad, I thought all their wishes seemed okay. It didn't seem like they were wishing for too much."

"I don't think so either. But when they got those wishes, it disrupted the order of things. They all thought they had found a shortcut to happiness without thinking about the cost. I totally believe wishes can come true, Kendyll. But it's more slow motion, like working over time to make a wish come true. Or waiting to grow to a certain point in life where you're ready to handle it. That's how you really do it."

"Not like gowns and slippers coming from a tree, huh, Dad?"

"You're right on point as usual," I laughed.

We drove on few more minutes and Kendyll was starting to look drowsy.

"It's funny about Cinderella and the tree," she said.

"What is?"

"Once when I was little you took me outside and the moon was out and you pointed across at the willows and you said they make you think of Mom because there was a little part of her in them because she loved them. Especially when the moon was shining on them."

"It's true; there's a trace of your Mom in everything she loved."

We drove a minute or two, and I had a sudden brainstorm.

"Hey, Kendyll! I wonder if that's what the Baker's Wife is talking about at the end. When she says let the baby see 'the glow.' I've never been quite sure what the glow is supposed to be. I wonder if it's a glow from her love, even though she herself is no longer there. What do you think?"

"I like that."

"You know, Kendyll. You and your Mom spent a lot of time together. She held you and kissed you and talked to you and just poured her love into you. And even though you don't remember her, that impression is inside you somewhere, giving off a little glow. I can see it in you every day. You will always have that in you."

"I know I will, Dad."

She sounded so small and so brave and I reached over and stroked her hair. We drove on quietly for a minute that

54

turned into a couple of minutes that turned into Kendyll being sound asleep.

***

"Dad? Should we go early tonight?"

"On closing night?" I said. "Most definitely."

When we got to the box office, we discovered the cast had left tickets for us. Everyone seemed eager to finish the run on a high note, and they were all wonderful and the time flew by. The last minutes came, and then "No One is Alone," and there were Cinderella and Red, sharing their quiet moment of comfort and understanding.

> **Hard to see the light now.**
> **Just don't let it go.**
> **Things will come out right now.**
> **We can make it so.**
> **Someone is on your side—**

I thought I noticed something odd about Cinderella's delivery. I looked closer and saw she wasn't wearing her usual Cinderella expression, but her normal Molly expression, and using her normal Molly voice and looking directly at Kendyll, like she had slipped out of character for a moment and was trying to communicate something to her, like 'this is the song I was talking about and I really want you to understand that we all are on your side here, and we believe things will come out right for you.' I gave a sidelong glance at Kendyll, and saw her locking gazes with Molly, eyes shining, nodding her head and looking very solemn.

After the performance, the stage manager came out and said, "Don't you two leave yet." Then Susan, Molly, Maryann, Bob, Sean, Karen and several others came out and gathered around us. They stood Kendyll up, and applauded as Susan made a little speech and presented her with her own cast gift. The joke was that the gift was a cast, a big green plaster cast model of the Giant's foot with a ribbon and inscriptions. They crowded around Kendyll and hugged her and shook my hand, wishing us luck and telling Kendyll they wouldn't be surprised to see her up on that stage some day. We hung around as long as we could, and finally had to accept it was all over.

Out on the highway, I waited for Kendyll to call the nightly roundup to order, but she didn't say a word. I looked over and she was sound asleep, scrunched against her pillow, hugging her green Giant's foot.

At home, I carried Kendyll in to bed, took the dog out and gave her water and a treat. I went into the living room, got my CD player and headphones, and lay down on the couch. I forwarded to the last exchange of dialogue in the show: the Baker and his spirit-tree Wife's last moments at the end.

"Just calm the child," she says.

I played the line over and over, remembering a beautiful fall morning, a gleaming white church, and a red maple tree at the height of its fall color.

"Just calm the child."

I was sitting at a table in a small conference room two days after Leslie's surgery. Sue, the head nurse of the neuro-ICU, was sitting down across from me. I had met with her many times in the last five days, and I started to wonder why she was taking so long to look me in the eye. She opened a binder and took out the file containing the pathology report from the surgery.

"Kevin, I think you would want me to get straight to the bottom line here."

"Yes, please."

"It's metastatic melanoma."

"It's the wrong file," I thought.

"Melanoma's a skin cancer, right? There's nothing on her skin."

"No, there isn't. This melanoma is non-cutaneous. It formed in Leslie's choroid. It's a layer of tissue that supplies blood to the back of the eye. The tumor went into her posterior fossa, at the base of the skull. That's what blocked circulation of her spinal fluid. Then it advanced into the brain stem."

"I've never heard of that."

"It's extremely rare. It usually affects people in their fifties or older. It's very rare for someone barely in their thirties. And even more unusual for it to spread to the brain. Leslie's symptoms were presenting so many false leads. Her pregnancy severely limited diagnostic options. But this would have been all the way down at the bottom of the list."

"How did it happen?"

"There is no known cause for this. It's just--"

Her hands were on the table and she clenched her fists really hard for a second, so hard they shook a little.

"We don't know," she said.

"Can they do anything?"

"The tumor isn't encapsulated. It's interwoven into her brain stem."

There must be a maximum survivable human pulse rate, but it turns out it's faster than I ever would have thought. It felt like being in a small room with a massive object I recognized as something I knew but couldn't quite put my finger on the name for.

"I guess this doesn't sound good."

Sue pushed the file aside and reached out and put a hand on my arm.

"There's no treatment for this, Kevin, except for palliative measures. Leslie is going to pass away."

"Okay. I guess I got that."

"I am so sorry."

"Do you know how long?"

"We can't really make predictions. But this is an aggressive, high grade cancer. It won't be very long. I promise you she'll be kept comfortable. She may recover enough from the surgery to be moved home. And maybe she'll be able to stay home all the way through. The next week will tell a lot. Your daughter is a little angel, Kevin. And Leslie is a very strong person. You guys will have some time to be a family. Someone from Social Services is waiting to meet with you whenever you're ready. You will have a lot of help available from really good people who really want to help you."

"Sue, you're sure about this, right?"

"Nobody wants to believe it, Kevin. It's just—"

She sighed and shook her head looking sad and weary and helpless.

"We are all so sorry."

It took some doing, but Sue and the hospital social workers convinced me that it would be best for Leslie if she could hear the news from me, and that the words would come to me and I couldn't mess it up because it wouldn't matter what I said if she wasn't ready to hear it. Her only outward reaction came when I told her of the possibility that we might be able to go home. She received this news with a welling of tears.

"Do you really think we could go home?" she asked.

"The way your incision is healing, it's entirely possible. It's going to be a beautiful fall. The trees are starting to turn. The maples are going to be so red with how dry it's been."

I remembered Leslie, surrounded by tubes and pumps and monitors, holding her healthy, beautiful baby, and looking her over carefully. When she was satisfied, she finally relaxed. I remembered arranging pillows into a nest to hold Kendyll in place on her mother, pulling her gown open and pulling the electrodes off her chest to let her baby smell her and feel her heartbeat.

After twelve days in Boston, Leslie was back in Portsmouth where she'd spent the summer. She started to become agitated, kept asking me questions, like from a checklist. She was very concerned, fighting to stay alert.

"Do we have firewood? Did Bob drop off the dresser? What about Kendyll's room?"

I had told her several times about waking up in Boston two weeks earlier, the morning after Kendyll was born, and remembering I had made plans to meet two friends to take care of a few small repairs on the house. But the transfer to

Boston came with about two hours notice, and I had never thought to call them and cancel. I tried to call them from the hospital and got answering machines. I tried the beach rental where my parents were staying. Finally I called my house in case anybody was waiting for me there. To my surprise, my dad answered the phone.

"How are they?"

"Good, Dad. There's nothing new since last night. Kendyll's with Leslie. You and Mom can see them both this afternoon. How is Mom?"

"So glad everyone is okay."

"Dad, can you help me out? I was supposed to meet Larry and Bob today and work on Kendyll's room. I never called them to cancel."

"They're here. They set up staging in the back, and they're up there building framing for the new windows."

"What new windows?"

"A truck just dropped three brand new windows in boxes in your driveway. I didn't think you had mentioned them, and I can't seem to get a straight answer on where they came from."

"Who's there?"

"It looks like half the town's here. Paula called us last night and I filled her in. She and Bob got on the phone. There are trucks parked all the way up the hill. There are table saws set up in the driveway and guys are cutting new siding for the back. I don't even know who most of these people are. They say they're friends of yours."

"What are they doing?"

"Well, Paula painted the bathroom and Jim put in a new shower, and Joe and Holly are putting up wallpaper in the kitchen. Kendyll's room is all torn apart. There are people all over the place. Somebody's coming in with a pile of pizza boxes, and somebody else just dumped a load of firewood in the yard."

But Leslie was still agitated about the house. She couldn't seem to remember I had told her this story. I bought some film, drove home, loaded up the camera, and walked all around. Then I had a one-hour photo place make an album.

"Here's Kendyll's room all painted with a new drop ceiling. Here's the dresser. Here's the crib. Here's the bathroom; seriously, that is our bathroom. Here's the firewood, all split and stacked. Here's the back of the house taken from up the hill. The new windows will keep it all nice and warm. Isn't it incredible? I'll leave the album right here by your bed."

Leslie closed the album and squeezed my hand.

"Thank you," she said. "Thank you."

Then she went to sleep, and never said another word about unfinished business. She was moved to a larger hospital in Dover, in the hope she might get symptom relief from radiation, although this proved unrealistic given the rapid course of her disease. Going home was not in the cards. The tumor started affecting her neurological function. She had seizures. Massive doses of steroids resulted in episodes of psychosis. One night she panicked and tried to rip out her lines until I pinned her down and hit the call button with my elbow. They restrained her until the drugs brought sleep and said it looked horrible but she wasn't really registering the experience or forming memories. I guess it wasn't the time to ask how the hell you can know that. One of the nurses took a plastic bag out of a cabinet and led me out into the hall.

"Leslie doesn't know you're here right now. She's not even on that stuff anymore. It's just working its way out of her system. She'll be herself in the morning. You want to be here for that. You're not resting enough. Go to the lounge and sleep, and we'll keep Kendyll right here next to her mom, and I promise we'll come get you if anything happens."

She handed me the plastic bag.

"Here's your pillow and blanket. Now, go! Go, or Kevin, I swear I'll get the game warden in here and take you down with a dart gun!"

And there I was laughing in the middle of a nightmare, and going off gratefully with my pillow and blanket for a few hours of desperately needed sleep.

Progressive doses of morphine kept the panic away as the tumor followed its predicted course and attacked Leslie's respiratory center. Then it was mostly peaceful, and Kendyll got to spend at least part of every day sleeping on her chest and feeling a mother's embrace. I truly believed she would always retain the impressions of these precious days with her mother.

I remembered Johnny, the gruff, burly ambulance driver, showing up outside her door with an arrangement of white roses. He had driven Leslie several times during her different transfers.

"These are from the crew. They couldn't figure out how someone in her situation could be so cheerful."

"She's always been an optimist," I said. "And she thinks you guys are good company."

"We get used to a lot of things," he said. "But this would just tear the heart out of you. We are so sorry."

Leslie was sleeping, so I gathered Kendyll up and took her out to say hello.

Johnny hesitated. "Do you think it would be all right if I held her for a second?"

I remembered the tears in his eyes, and how gently he kissed Kendyll's forehead.

"God love you, honey," he murmured.

Leslie's oldest friends travelled from different parts of the country to see her and fuss over Kendyll. Her best friend from childhood had a delayed flight and arrived at a busy time. She peeked in through the door, past a small group of family and friends, got a glimpse of Leslie, and turned back and leaned against the wall outside, weeping quietly. Then she dried her tears and marched in and entertained everyone with wonderful stories about their exploits at Lower Merion High School.

"Plug your ears, Kendyll!" she said.

Leslie wasn't speaking too much by then, but she certainly hadn't lost her ability to enjoy a good laugh. I cleared the room so they could be alone, and when Amanda came out, I knew I had seen an unforgettable display of courage.

Finally I remembered the night. Actually really thought about it. Turning down the lights, sitting quietly, occasionally mentioning that everything was fine at home, or how Kendyll was safe at my folks sleeping in her crib, or how nice it is to drift off to sleep when you're really tired. Leaving the room frequently and giving her time alone in case that was her preference. Holding her and whispering, "it's time to take care of yourself." And after she'd finally found her moment, I was going out into the hall and being met by a cluster of nurses, all crowded there right when I first opened the door, who surrounded me and hugged me and held my hands.

"We're so sorry. Do you want anything? Do you want us to make some calls for you? There's no hurry. You just stay until you feel ready to leave."

The oncologist arrived to make it official, embracing me, his face full of sorrow.

"You did good, man," he whispered.

"Thanks for taking care of her pain," I replied. "Really, thanks. Keep doing that."

Meg and Dave arrived around midnight to drive me home. I looked back into the room and felt no reluctance to leave. Leslie's spirit was far away from her suffering.

Lying there on the couch, listening to *Into the Woods*, I finally felt it after seven years of trying to run from it. Carrying a three-week-old baby girl wrapped in a pink blanket into the gleaming white church up the hill from our house, the great bell slowly tolling, the church packed with mourners. I remembered the stir in the air as I carried Kendyll down the aisle.

"Just calm the child."

I remembered the red maple tree outside the window nearest me, at the peak of its autumn color. I had been right about the dry weather. The maple was practically singing in the bright sun. It was red like I've never seen red before or since. I bowed my head and looked back and forth between the sleeping Kendyll and that beautiful blazing maple tree.

Then the wonderful Reverend Howes got up and said:

"Three years ago, many of us came together in this place to celebrate the union of Leslie and Kevin in the bonds of marriage."

Then he looked out over all our heads for the longest time.

"Well," he said softly, "today we are here again."

And as I remembered, my defenses were overrun once and for all. The rising panic I had tamped down the first night Kendyll and I went to the show came rushing back and rose up and issued forth in an explosive discharge.

"Come and get me! What are you gonna do? Hurt me? You can't hurt me! I'm ready for you! I'm not running away anymore! I'm sick of running!"

And finally the tears came. Waves of pain poured out of my eyes, streaming down my temples, soaking my hair, soaking the pillow under my head. I noticed that when I breathed in, the flow of tears seemed to subside. Then I noticed the slower I exhaled, the more it seemed to turn up the faucet. I tried to trace where these waves of pain were coming from, a place so deep down that I had never known it existed, a place where I had held my pain and sorrow at such catastrophic loss and suffering, and the rage that had seeped through to my heart's core and festered there and befouled my spirit. Then I gave up on the breathing tricks and it all came pouring and pouring out, and for once I didn't try to stop it, and with that blissful surrender came the first nascent stirrings of new life, stirring inside me like the first seedlings of spring, peeking through the ashen earth of a once-proud forest ravaged by fire and left to waste until cleansed and nourished by the sweet rains of release.

***

The next day was Labor Day. Kendyll didn't skip into my room at the crack of dawn. We slept really late. School started the following morning, so we spent the day outside getting our last taste of summer. We took Ceili for a long walk in the woods. We went to the beach. We rode our bikes. We kind of floated through the day. We didn't see anybody. We didn't listen to any music. We didn't talk about *Into the Woods*, although I suspect we both felt the loss. We went for an ice cream cone after dinner, and, when we got back, I started cleaning up the kitchen.

Kendyll was in her room with the *Into the Woods* CD playing on her boom box. I brought in some clean laundry, and saw she had her new clothes and school supplies arranged on her bed. She was sorting through them, singing along with the music, having a fine time. I did notice one thing. Her locket with Leslie's picture she usually kept hanging on her bedpost was sitting open on the bed.

Twenty minutes later I was doing the dishes.

"Dad?"

Her voice was tiny and quavering. I looked around and she was leaning in the doorway, hugging herself, locket in hand, tears streaming down her face. I turned off the water and grabbed a towel. She was not looking good.

"What's wrong?"

"Why can't I have my Mom?"

I picked her up, and she let go in a torrent of crying. I carried her into the living room, sat on the couch, and held her on my lap, rocking her as she buried her face in my chest, sobbing. The fury of her outpouring increased and she pounded my chest with her fists.

*"Why can't I have my Mom? Why can't I have my*

71

*Mom?"*

I had been told all along she would eventually experience some kind of grief process. I was told by her pediatrician, a couple of hospice counselors, a couple of social workers, and pretty much everything I had read. And the thought always made me queasy.

Everyone said I would know what to do, but I thought what else would they say? I tried to give her every chance. I didn't shy away from the subject. I read books to her about leaves falling off trees and stuff. I read myself books about helping children suffering from grief with books about leaves falling off trees and stuff. I stayed in touch with Leslie's friends and dragged Kendyll all over the place to see them. I told her stories about her mother, including one as we decorated our Christmas tree. We'd bring our tree home, and I'd set it up in the living room and bring down the box of decorations. We'd string up the lights, and Kendyll would take out a smaller green cardboard box, place it carefully on the coffee table, and sit on the couch.

"Okay."

"What?"

"Aren't you going to tell me about the rag bows?"

"Oh, Kendyll. You know all about the rag bows."

"Dad!"

I'd sit down with her.

"Okay. Your Mom and I were just starting out, and we didn't have a lot of money. Christmas was coming, and we only had a few ornaments because your Mom only had room for a small tree in her apartment, and I never bothered with a Christmas tree. We couldn't really afford to buy more decorations, because we had just bought the house and stretched ourselves pretty thin moneywise to do it. So your Mom got a bunch of gold calico rags someplace, and tore them into strips, and fashioned them, just like she would design a beautiful jacket or dress, into these beautiful little rag bows. Then we got the biggest tree we could fit in the house, and put the rags bows all over it. And your Mom lit a bunch of candles in the room, and we sat right here and thought it was the most wonderful, old-fashioned Christmas tree that was ever seen. But there was still something missing. We loved each other so much, but we knew there was room in the house for a lot more love. So—"

"Yeah?"

"We got the dog."

"Hey!"

"You know what happened. We ended up with more love in our lives than we ever could have dreamed of. And that's why we're sitting here talking about the rag bows."

I gave her a hug and kissed her forehead.

"Let's get decorating!"

Then we'd put the bows on the tree. It's not Dickens or anything, but I was desperate for family rituals, especially around the holidays, to give her a sense of continuity and belonging. Nothing dramatic ever happened, but I figured I was doing what I could. And, as years passed, I started gradually letting it slide until I never thought much about the question of Kendyll's supposedly inevitable grieving.

I thought of all that and more sitting there holding the weeping Kendyll. Then it struck me that we'd been sitting there for a while. Then it came to a point where I started wondering how long I should let her go on without trying to intervene somehow. This wasn't in any of the books. Kendyll went to a very dark place that night, and the burden she expelled seemed far more than her brave young soul could have carried for so long. I just held on to her and tried to stay calm. I wiped her tears and brushed her hair off her face and kept whispering it was okay. When she had finally worn herself out, I kissed her and held up tissues for her to blow her nose.

Kendyll finally fell asleep. I carried her to bed and paced around the house in distress, repeatedly going in to check on her. I couldn't imagine she was going to be in any shape to go to school.

"I let this happen," I thought.

When I woke her in the morning, she looked wrung out.

"Are you okay?"

"Yes."

"Do you feel well enough to get up?"

"Sure."

"Do you think you can make school?"

"I'm really okay, Dad."

I got her on the bus and went immediately to the phone. I called the counselor at her school, and she told me to swing by right before lunch. I had done some volunteering at the school the previous two years, and I knew Kathy pretty well and had a lot of respect for her opinion. I had met her the day of Kendyll's kindergarten registration, when I stopped in her office and announced, "My daughter and I are in a unusual situation, and I might need some help."

"And you will have it," she said, cheerfully.

We sat in her office and I told her the story of our journey into the woods and Kendyll's situation the night before.

"I think I've made a real mess of this," I said. "I was getting really scared for her last night."

"Well, that must have been very upsetting," said Kathy.

"You sound just like a counselor."

"I know, but it really must have. That would freak me out a little."

"Oh, great."

"Kevin, I think it's wonderful that Kendyll has found a way to express her sorrow."

"I don't know what I was thinking," I said. "I'm supposed to be the parent. I wished I'd scooped her up and taken her out of there the first night. I should have anticipated this."

I eventually noticed I wasn't giving Kathy a chance to say anything. I snapped out of it and looked at her.

"Kevin."

"Yeah, sorry."

"I'm glad to hear all this."

"Are you kidding me?"

"This was good. Kendyll knew it was important. She related the issues in the show to her own life. It was safe because it was about other people. And the acceptance and kindness you received night after night from the people at the show reinforced that feeling of safety. It had a cumulative effect. It was like they created a little sanctuary for you. They just sound like wonderful people."

"They really were."

"This was a great situation. That show was exactly what both of you needed. And it was a musical, which would heighten the emotions that were there anyway, and lower your defenses even more. Catharsis isn't just a word from English class. It translates to 'purification,' meaning getting rid of bad, nasty, poisonous things."

"I guess that makes sense."

"Seriously, Kevin. People have a way of ending up where they need to be. Kendyll's instincts were taking her exactly where she needed to go. She just needed you to drive her to Boston."

"You're funny."

"After you called, I went down to her classroom to look in on her, and I checked in with Nancy, and Kendyll is perfectly fine. She's a great kid, Kevin. You are doing just fine with her. Some day you'll see this crisis as the beginning of her healing."

We talked some more, and I thanked Kathy and went home thinking she might be on to something. I decided to keep an eye on Kendyll and maybe everything would be okay. Her seventh birthday came along two weeks later. I had been studying her minutely the whole time for any hint of anything. And all I could see was one very happy looking kid.

*\*\*\**

A couple of months after our journey into the woods, I got a call from the historical museum in our town. They wanted me to team up with a guy named Steven Mallory to create a music program for a series they were doing in the gleaming white church up the hill from my house. I had worked with Steven on another project for the museum a year or so before. Our preparations for this new music program involved working closely with the museum's public relations director, one Cheryl St. Germain. I'd never actually met her, but I'd seen her frequently in the local newspapers, presenting an award to some designer from the show house, or posing with hard hat and shovel along with her fellow Chamber of Commerce directors.

One day in January, I went up the hill to the museum library to meet with Cheryl and Steven, and start putting the program together. We sat at a conference table, passing pages back and forth and scribbling notes.

"Okay," I said. "It's 1753, and for many years the tragic figure of the Reverend Handkerchief Moody has hidden behind his black veil, bound by a vow of silence. Late one night, his landlord is shocked to hear him singing in his bedchamber. And sometime during the night, his voice is stilled forever. And his last words are a song called "O For An Overcoming Faith to Ease My Dying Hour.'"

"Isaac Watts," said Steven. "I'll make a copy."

"So one of us tells the story, and the other sings?"

"Like a cross-fade?" said Steven.

"Nice!"

I looked at my notes.

"Cheryl? When Mark Twain gave his speech for the 250th, didn't he quote from a song?"

"'Let Children Hear the Mighty Deeds.'" replied Cheryl. "A chorus of school kids sang it after the speech."

"Watts again," said Steven. "And kind of inspiring."

"The organ over there is pretty amazing. If I sing it, could you play it on the organ with a lot of flourish and fireworks?"

"I'll totally overdo it."

"Cheryl, can we get a copy of the speech?"

"There aren't any known copies. But we have a book of clippings with some quotes," said Cheryl, jotting a note on her pad.

"Oh," she added. "Longfellow used to stay at Freeman's Tavern out on Post Road, when he was traveling between Portland and Boston. He played his flute with a fiddle player called Black Isaac Davis, and tipped him three cents a tune. We have a pamphlet with the names of some of the tunes. And an article about him trying to use his flute to converse with birds."

Our music program was off to a good start. One day, Steven and I were working in the library, and Cheryl stopped in to drop off some clippings. The three of us chatted for a few minutes, and Cheryl went on her way.

"What do you think?" asked Steven.

"About what?"

"What do you think of Cheryl?"

"What do you mean?"

"I'll bet she would go out with you."

"Geez, Steven. What is this, high school?"

One Friday afternoon, I went up to Cheryl's office to help her finish up the press releases and select photos of Steven and me for the poster and local papers. We sat together at her desk. It was the first time we had been alone. We sat talking in muted tones, our elbows practically touching.

"Here's a good one." I said.

"Hmm."

"What?"

"Funny hair thing going on. Here's one."

"My eyes look totally demented!"

"That's the great thing about it."

I had learned a few things about Cheryl in the previous couple of weeks. I had known she was a striking, sparkly, witty single mother of three, and a person of exceptional determination and character, who had traveled a difficult path of her own. And I learned that the challenges of her situation, a demanding job, two boys in their early teens and a preschool daughter, juggling various projects and commitments in the community, seemed to have no effect on her sunny outlook. That she always looked for the best in any person or situation. And suddenly, I heard a voice that sounded a lot like mine asking her out.

Her house was a neat little shingled ranch in a stand of pines. I pulled up in front and sat for a minute. I suddenly realized this was a date. I had no idea how long it had been since I'd gone on an actual date.

"I feel like I'm twenty," I thought. "Like I'm trying to get up the nerve to talk to some girl at the Book Port."

As an eager twenty-year-old, I started to get the idea that the world held broader horizons than the all-night hot dog stand where I had worked my way through school. All the free food I could eat and hours of quiet reading in the middle of the night no longer satisfied my creative impulses.

A half-hour down the road, on the square in Kennebunkport, was a bookstore called the Kennebunk Book Port. It occupied the loft of a rum warehouse built in 1775, and boasted a selection that leaned toward the literary and offbeat, a comfortable sofa, a friendly black cat named Lucifer, and a customer base with a high concentration of pretty, artistic young women. So I wrote a letter.

"This letter has to be the best thing I ever wrote," I thought.

I sent the letter, and the owners made a phone call to a person who taught writing classes at my school. I eventually came to be friends with her family. Her husband was pastor of the historic church in Kennebunkport, and eleven years later, would come down and perform the ceremony on the day Leslie and I were joined in marriage. She's in her eighties now. I saw them both recently at one of her poetry readings, and thanked her once again for returning that phone call to the Book Port. I'll see them again in a couple of weeks, to celebrate his 90th.

I worked at the Book Port for four years. I loved unlocking the door every morning, stepping in and smelling the distinctive tang of 200-year-old wood and listening for the ghosts of the sailors whose 200-year-old graffiti adorned the wooden beams overhead. But as much as I loved working in the store, it was the deck out back that became my place of dreaming.

The deck had three levels, reached by sets of winding wooden stairs. It had benches, a couple of Adirondack chairs, and, dozens of flowerpots and boxes overflowing with thousands of bright, fragrant flowers, trailing down toward the water.

The view from the deck consisted of other similar buildings grouped around the tidal water, perched on their wood pilings. One had a green awning and a green wood-carved sign and small-paned wooden patio doors. In the background was the top of a yellow clapboard house with green shutters and twin brick chimneys, set against a backdrop of trees.

On that deck, I sat and thought deep thoughts, practiced my guitar, and wished, more than anything, for a life that would be interesting. And at no point did I ever think of my mother's cheery admonition to be careful what I wished for.

I got out of the car and rang the doorbell. Cheryl opened the door.

"I'm just getting the kids squared away. Come in for a second."

I stamped the snow off my feet, and stepped into the front hall, as Cheryl went to deal with the kids. I closed the door, and looked to my left. There on the wall, about two feet from my face, was a framed watercolor. It depicted a half-dozen old wooden buildings sitting on pilings over the water. The buildings had decks with benches and flowerpots and winding sets of wooden stairs. One building had a green awning and a green wood-carved sign and small-paned wooden patio doors. In the background was the top of a yellow clapboard house with green shutters and twin brick chimneys. The whole scene was set against a backdrop of trees.

I stared at the painting. I knew every detail, the weather beaten old buildings, every railing and piling as familiar to me as my own living room.

"I'm ready to go."

I wheeled around and there was Cheryl.

"Where did you get this painting?"

"I bought that a long time ago, when I first moved here. This deck is behind this amazing bookstore in Kennebunkport. I went in and sat on the couch and petted the cat, and read for a while, and I didn't want to leave. The place just felt so comfortable. Then I saw this in the window of a gallery. I couldn't really afford it, but I bought it anyway. So you must know where this is."

"I worked there for four years."

"In Kennebunkport?"

"In the bookstore."

We stood staring at each other. Then we went to dinner and fell in love. After three years, we decided to throw statistical probability to the wind and take the plunge and take our chances with all these kids and all the baggage, and see how long we could make it last. We're up to fifteen years now. The kids are all out on their own, so mostly it's just us and our dog, Rosa. But we get together with any and all of the kids at every opportunity.

Kendyll is twenty-five as of this writing, and she has grown up to far surpass her early exceptional promise. She still possesses an uncanny degree of insight. Her perceptions are acute, her expressions are elegant, her heart is of the purest, and her spirit is of the most spirited. She does the highest honor to Leslie's memory with her grace, compassion, creativity and great inner strength. She always acts in a way that would make her mother proud.

Kendyll never knew Leslie, so her real loss was that of a life that would never be--the sisters or brothers she would never have, the unique intimacy and love of the mother she would never know, the warmth and security of having a close-knit family with a strong sense of continuity and belonging. Now Kendyll could have a new life that would be, with a beloved younger sister and two protective older brothers, three sets of wonderful grandparents and a bunch of aunts, uncles and cousins to match. And, most recently, she has a completely adorable new nephew. She has childhood memories of a lively, bustling family home, with people going in and out all the time, extra kids rotating in and out, spirited discussions at the kitchen counter, doors slamming, sharing triumphs and trials, games, meets, lessons, parents nights, camps, concerts, plays and recitals, the annual ritual of packing the minivan with kids, bikes and surfboards for summer vacations at our usual ramshackle, leaky old rental house on our favorite island hideaway. Not to mention the part about having a loving Mom with whom she traveled into the woods of the "mother/daughter thing," much like any mother and daughter, and emerged the best of friends. The two of them now share a close and intimate bond they will cherish for the rest of their lives.

Cheryl left the museum eight years ago to do marketing and public relations for an historic summer theatre that does musicals. I know things now. Like that Stephen Sondheim is way overdue for that fun kids musical. As you might guess, I go to the theatre a lot more than I used to. Sometimes I notice someone in the audience reacting in a way that draws my attention and makes me wonder if they might be on some kind of journey into their own dark and scary woods. I always wish I could reach out and put my hand on their arm and wish them the best on their path through darkness.

> **Hard to see the light now.**
> **Just don't let it go.**
> **Things will come out right now.**
> **We can make it so.**

## Someone is on your side—

When I think back to that magical summer production of *Into the Woods,* I feel great admiration for the many people who brought the show to life. James Lapine wrote the mother of all fairy tales--emotionally complex, vastly entertaining and equally accessible to an almost seven-year-old and an almost grown-up single father. Stephen Sondheim took this treasure trove of material and created music to cast a spell like Orpheus with his golden lyre--a beacon to guide lost sailors and theatre-goers past the Sirens of grief and pain, along with words to amuse, move, enlighten and inspire. And in certain cases, to weep violently. Catharsis is not just a word from English class.

Since Cheryl has been in the business of theatre, I have learned a lot about what it takes to mount a big musical--how many talented, dedicated people, onstage and off, and how incredibly hard they work. I know how idealistic and determined they are, and that a life in theatre isn't an easy one. My gratitude and admiration go out to all these people, and especially those who reached out so kindly and generously to help Kendyll and me on our path through the woods, while simultaneously navigating the twists and turns of their own life journeys. I hope that theatre artists everywhere understand how much good they can bring to the world via their craft and chosen profession. And I wish they might all live happily ever after.

The End

## Acknowledgements:

Stephen Sondheim and James Lapine, for their generosity, genius, and inspiration.

Eric and Judith Angelson, without whom this would be a story that was never told.

Neil McMahon for cover design.

Rick Pappas, for "clearing" the way.

Molly Beck Ferguson, our brave Cinderella, for her kind and good nature and prodigious memory.

Kathy Welch, for caring and counseling.

Jayme McDaniel, a wonderful theatre artist, whose wisest advice to me wasn't about theatre.

Jan Brennan and Don Wessels, tough editors, great friends.

Anyone and everyone involved with the Publick Theatre's 1996 production of INTO THE WOODS.

My sisters, Ann and Meg, and their spouses, Tom and Dave, for bearing the unbearable.

Kelsey, Nolan, Travis, and Justin for being my wonderful family.

Cheryl Farley, for my happily ever after.

And my beautiful Kendyll.